WITHDRAWN

DATE			

ELMOLO

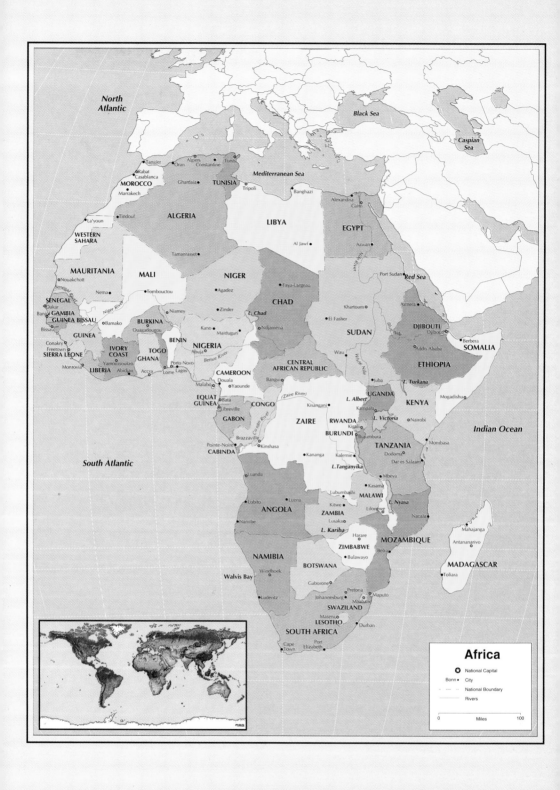

North
Atlantic

Black Sea

Caspian
Sea

Tangier
Algiers
Oran Constantine Tunis
Rabat
Casablanca
MOROCCO
Marrakech
Ghardaia
TUNISIA
Mediterranean Sea
Tripoli
Banghazi
Alexandria
Cairo

La'youn
Tindouf
ALGERIA
LIBYA
EGYPT

WESTERN
SAHARA
Tamanrasset
Al Jawf
Aswan

MAURITANIA
MALI
NIGER
CHAD
Faya-Largeau
Port Sudan
Red Sea

Nouakchott
Nema
Tombouctou
Agadez
L. Chad
Khartoum
Asmera
DJIBOUTI
Djibouti

SENEGAL
Dakar
Niamey
Zinder
Ndjamena
El Fasher
SUDAN
Addis Ababa
Berbera
SOMALIA

GAMBIA
Banjul
GUINEA BISSAU
Bamako
BURKINA
Ouagadougou
Kano
Maiduguri
Wau
White Nile
ETHIOPIA

Bissau
GUINEA
BENIN
NIGERIA
Abuja
CENTRAL
AFRICAN REPUBLIC
Juba
L. Turkana

Conakry
Freetown
SIERRA LEONE
IVORY
COAST
TOGO
GHANA
Benue River
L. Albert
UGANDA
KENYA
Mogadishu

Monrovia
LIBERIA
Abidjan
Accra
Porto Novo
Lagos
CAMEROON
Douala
Yaounde
Bangui
Kampala
Nairobi
Indian Ocean

EQUAT
GUINEA
Bata
Malabo
(Zaire River)
Kisangani
L. Victoria
Mombasa

GABON
Libreville
CONGO
ZAIRE
RWANDA
Kigali
BURUNDI
Bujumbura
TANZANIA
Dodoma

South Atlantic
Brazzaville
Pointe-Noire
Kinshasa
CABINDA
Kananga
Kalemie
Dar es Salaam

Luanda
L. Tanganyika
Mbeya

Lobito
Luena
Lubumbashi
Kasama

Kitwe
MALAWI
L. Nyasa
Nacala

Namibe
ANGOLA
ZAMBIA
Lusaka
Lilongwe

L. Kariba
Harare
MOZAMBIQUE
Mahajanga

NAMIBIA
ZIMBABWE
Beira
Antananarivo

Walvis Bay
BOTSWANA
Bulawayo
MADAGASCAR

Windhoek
Gaborone
Pretoria
Maputo
Toliara

Ludenitz
Johannesburg
Mbabane

SWAZILAND
Maseru
LESOTHO
Durban

SOUTH AFRICA
Cape
Town
Port
Elizabeth

Africa

- ✪ National Capital
- Bonn • City
- – – – National Boundary
- ——— Rivers

0   Miles   100

The Heritage Library of African Peoples

ELMOLO

Ursula Gaertner, Ph.D.

THE ROSEN PUBLISHING GROUP, INC.
NEW YORK

Published in 1995 by The Rosen Publishing Group, Inc.
29 East 21st Street, New York, NY 10010

First Edition

Manufactured in the United States of America

Library of Congress Cataloging-in-Publication Data

Gaertner, Ursula.
 Elmolo / Ursula Gaertner. — 1st ed.
  p. cm. — (The Heritage library of African peoples)
 Includes bibliographical references and index.
 ISBN 0-8239-1764-9
 1. Elmolo (African people)—Juvenile literature. I. Title.
II. Series.
DT433.545.E45G34 1995
967.62′7—dc20   94-29587
                 CIP
                 AC

Contents

INTRODUCTION

THERE IS EVERY REASON FOR US TO KNOW something about Africa and to understand its past and the way of life of its peoples. Africa is a rich continent that has for centuries provided the world with art, culture, labor, wealth, and natural resources. It has vast mineral deposits, fossil fuels, and commercial crops.

But perhaps most important is the fact that fossil evidence indicates that human beings originated in Africa. The earliest traces of human beings and their tools are almost two million years old. Their descendants have migrated throughout the world. To be human is to be of African descent.

The experiences of the peoples who stayed in Africa are as rich and as diverse as of those who established themselves elsewhere. This series of books describes their environment, their modes of subsistence, their relationships, and their customs and beliefs. The books present the variety of languages, histories, cultures, and religions that are to be found on the African continent. They demonstrate the historical linkages between African peoples and the way contemporary Africa has been affected by European colonial rule.

Africa is large, complex, and diverse. It encompasses an area of more than 11,700,000

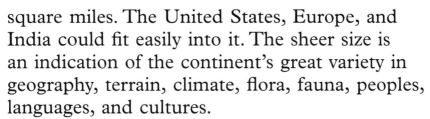

square miles. The United States, Europe, and India could fit easily into it. The sheer size is an indication of the continent's great variety in geography, terrain, climate, flora, fauna, peoples, languages, and cultures.

Much of contemporary Africa has been shaped by European colonial rule, industrialization, urbanization, and the demands of a world economic system. For more than seventy years, large regions of Africa were ruled by Great Britain, France, Belgium, Portugal, and Spain. African peoples from various ethnic, linguistic, and cultural backgrounds were brought together to form colonial states.

For decades Africans struggled to gain their independence. It was not until after World War II that the colonial territories became independent African states. Today, almost all of Africa is ruled by Africans. Large numbers of Africans live in modern cities. Rural Africa is also being transformed, and yet its people still engage in many of their age-old customs and beliefs.

Contemporary circumstances and natural events have not always been kind to ordinary Africans. Today, however, new popular social movements and technological innovations pose great promise for future development.

George C. Bond
Institute of African Studies
Columbia University, New York City

Through cleverness and courage, the Elmolo have survived their difficult environment, largely by fishing.

chapter

1

THE PEOPLE OF
THE LAKE

THE ELMOLO LIVE ON THE SOUTHEASTERN
shore of Lake Turkana in northern Kenya.
Although their population is only about 250,
the Elmolo have attracted considerable attention
for their unique way of life. Through cleverness
and courage, they are able to live in a difficult,
unfriendly environment.

Not much is known about Elmolo history. It
is thought that they may have been part of the
Rendille people at some point in the distant
past. They do have some language and cultural
traits in common with the Rendille. Over the
past few hundred years, however, the Elmolo
have created an individual culture and they are
very different now from their neighbors the
Rendille, the Samburu, and the Turkana.

These neighbors are pastoralists; that is,
animal herders. The Elmolo live by fishing and
by hunting water and land animals. They are

experts in the use of log rafts, from which they harpoon or spear large fish, turtles, and the enormous Nile crocodile. For the Elmolo, a life without fishing is unthinkable.

Long ago, the Elmolo lived on small offshore islands that dotted the shoreline of Lake Turkana, providing protection against raiders from the north and east. Over the past hundred years, and especially in the last thirty or forty, much has changed. The Elmolo now live in two villages. The smaller and more traditional one is on Lorian Island in Elmolo Bay. The larger one is a few miles from the small oasis town of Loiyangalani, "The Place of Trees."

The inhabitants of the mainland settlement have adopted many cultural practices from their pastoralist neighbors, as well as from Europeans who have come to Loiyangalani. Marked differences have developed between the island community and the mainland Elmolo, who have incorporated monetary values. Both communities have largely abandoned their original language in favor of Sampur (Samburu). Although the Elmolo have adopted some of the practices of other cultures, their own beliefs, values, and patterns of relationship remain to ensure their survival as a distinct cultural group.

▼ ORAL TRADITION ▼

Before the arrival of Europeans, the Elmolo

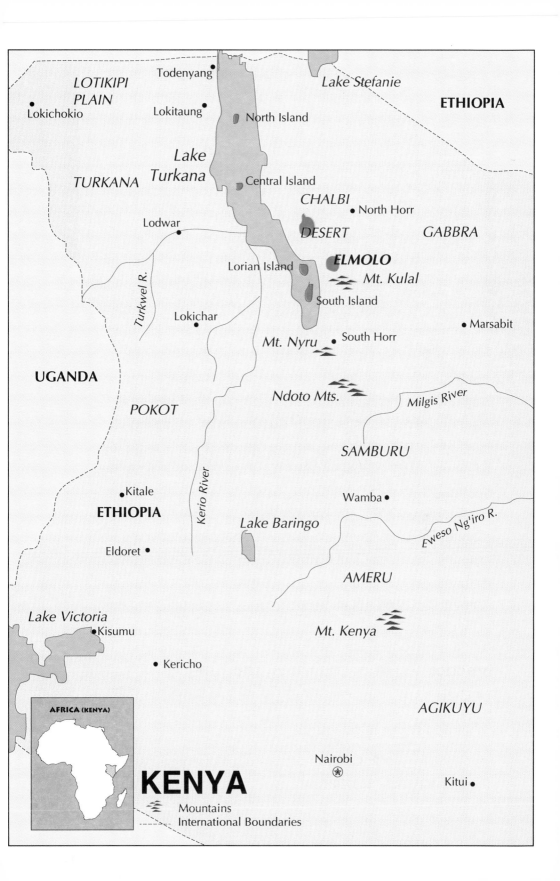

A group of Elmolo fishing with nets.

had no written language. Knowledge was passed on by word of mouth. This is called oral tradition. Grandparents and parents told their children stories of the past. According to these stories, the Elmolo have always lived on the lake and were never part of another group of people. They were proud of their different way of life and language. They told their children legends that taught them right from wrong and explained the reasons for certain customs.

European anthropologists tried to test the truth of these stories by questioning the Elmolo and their neighbors and by observing their activities over time. Physical evidence of settlements, such as bones, tools, and the ashes from old cooking fires, was also used. In this way a view of the Elmolo as a people was developed.

▼ ORIGIN OF THE NAME ▼

No one is sure about the origin of the name Elmolo. Perhaps it originated from *o-mouo*, the word for "fisherman" in the Cushitic language subfamily. Or from *mo-lo*, which means "this person" in the original Elmolo language. In their own language, they called themselves, *gura paua*, "The People of the Lake."

The pastoralist neighbors of the Elmolo regard any person who does not own cattle—or, in the case of the Rendille, camels—as poor and destitute. A poor person is to be pitied or destroyed. People like the Elmolo who fish and hunt for their livelihood are therefore called *il torobo*, Maasai for poor beggars. This name was given to more than a dozen groups, including the Elmolo, that lived on the slopes of the Rift Valley and did not own livestock.

When the first European travelers reached the eastern shore of Lake Turkana, they asked some cattle-herders, "Who are those people who fish on the lake?" The herders replied, "Those are Elmolo." From that time on, the fishermen on the lake were referred to as Elmolo in all European reports.

▼ LAKE DWELLERS ▼

This incorrect assumption led to many misconceptions about the peoples who made their living by fishing on Lake Turkana. On occasion,

An Elmolo girl with her daily food, a Nile perch.

The Elmolo survive by fishing. This man prepares his net.

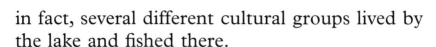

in fact, several different cultural groups lived by the lake and fished there.

The first were members of the Samburu tribe who had lost all their cattle in a devastating plague in the 1880s. Having no animals, they turned to fishing and hunting to survive. Most of these people returned to cattle-herding when conditions improved.

The second group of fishermen were the Dassenech. These were people from the Reshiat or Merille tribes who customarily lived at the northern end of Lake Turkana, where the Omo River flows from Ethiopia into the lake. At certain times of the year, the Dassenech came as far south as Alia Bay to fish, then returned to their permanent homes.

Finally there was an earlier generation, the Elmolo of today. These people have remained attached to one area and one form of economy year-round and have lived on the lake for several hundred years. Over the centuries, they have developed their own culture, language, traditions, customs, and social organization. When first encountered by Europeans in the 1890s, Elmolo elders insisted that they were a distinct group, quite separate from their neighbors, with different lifestyles and customs. They were *gura paua*, "The People of the Lake." These then, are the people we mean when we speak of Elmolo.▲

chapter

2

THE LAND

LAKE TURKANA WAS FORMED MILLIONS OF years ago. At that time, the area was well watered and fertile, with large forests and many animals. But the earth's crust in that region was very unstable. From time to time, the liquid rock of the earth's core forced its way to the surface in spectacular volcanic eruptions. Over the next twenty million years, successive layers of lava, sediment, and volcanic ash were deposited on the crust, so that the whole region now looks like the surface of the moon.

The turbulence below the earth's crust also caused shifts as the cooling outer layers adjusted to inner forces of pressure and heat. The ground quaked and moved. The earth's crust broke in numerous places along a north-south line. Land was lifted up in some areas, and dropped in others. These movements created a long trench

17

The Elmolo have made the most of their arid climate by looking to the lake for sustenance.

One of two Elmolo villages on the hot, dry shore of Lake Turkana.

with smaller cracks running along it to the east and west. The trench, called the East African Rift Valley, extends hundreds of miles from north to south.

The land is dotted with volcanic cinder cones. Rock outcrops and hills rise up here and there. Only a few shrubby plants grow in this difficult environment. It was in this area that the earliest fossils of humans, their tools, and the animals they hunted were found in the 1980s. These fossils are 2 to 3 million years old.

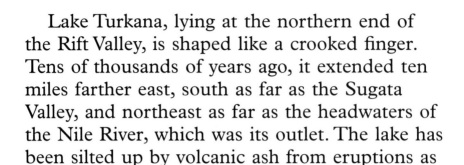

Lake Turkana, lying at the northern end of the Rift Valley, is shaped like a crooked finger. Tens of thousands of years ago, it extended ten miles farther east, south as far as the Sugata Valley, and northeast as far as the headwaters of the Nile River, which was its outlet. The lake has been silted up by volcanic ash from eruptions as well as by erosion of the surrounding land.

The climate of the area is hot and dry. Over the past century, the water level has dropped by more than one foot a year. The receding waters exposed large areas of land, and the lake's outlet to the Nile River system was cut off. Now only one permanent river remains, the Omo at the northern end. Since the Omo River is fed by rains, the water level of the lake depends on rainfall in the north. Seen from a distance, Lake Turkana has an opaque, dark green appearance. The Maasai called it *Embasso Narok*, or the "Black Lake." Later travelers called it the "The Jade Sea."

▼ THE ISLANDS ▼

Three major lava rock islands jut out from the lake: North Island, Center Island, and South Island. Vegetation is sparse. Center Island has three lakes, where crocodiles breed.

The Turkana people have a legend about a time when the south end of the lake was totally dry and a group of people made their home on the island. One morning they awoke to find themselves surrounded by water, stranded on the island. The Turkana tell how campfires glowed on the island's western shore in the evening, but one by one the fires disappeared until none were left.

No one believed the Turkana story until British explorers W.S. Dyson and V.E. Fuchs discovered animal and human bones on the island as well as ashes from campfires in 1935.

The Lake Turkana region has two rainy seasons and two dry seasons. The big rains come between March and May, and the small rains are expected from October to December. The small rains are unpredictable, however, and often fail to materialize, leaving the region to the merciless sun and winds. The area south of Alia Bay receives less than 10 inches of rain a year.

The amount of rainfall is only half the story; how the rains fall is also important. If they come in torrential downpours, the water simply washes away and fails to replenish the ground. Small streams become roaring washes, and the water takes with it everything in its path. At such times, the streams cannot be crossed. If the rains fall in a gentler fashion, the water has a chance to seep deeply into the earth.

After the rains, a belt of grass appears on the eastern shore of the lake and in patches here and there where pools of water remain. Beyond that, the rocky ground and the terrible heat make plant life almost impossible. The only

This young girl wears a *selah*, a "dressing net" made from fiber strings of the doum palm.

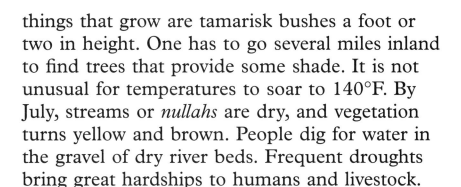

things that grow are tamarisk bushes a foot or two in height. One has to go several miles inland to find trees that provide some shade. It is not unusual for temperatures to soar to 140°F. By July, streams or *nullahs* are dry, and vegetation turns yellow and brown. People dig for water in the gravel of dry river beds. Frequent droughts bring great hardships to humans and livestock.

Lake Turkana is approximately 123 feet above sea level. It is 155 miles long from north to south and 35 miles across at its widest point. The lake is much deeper in the south, reaching 450 feet; in the north it reaches a depth of only 30 feet. The water is slightly salty; the greater the depth, the less salty is the water.

▼ THE CHALBI DESERT ▼

Old volcanic cones dot the shoreline, and their peaks can be seen along the horizon. Mt. Kulal, at the southeastern edge of the lake, rises to over 7,500 feet. A forest of cedars and olive trees covers its slopes, in sharp contrast to the surrounding lava wastelands. Mt. Kulal overlooks the stony and barren Chalbi Desert to the east and north as far as the eye can see. The mountain has been blamed for the sudden windstorms that whip down its flanks off the town of Loiyangalani. The wind may reach 60 miles an hour and turn the lake into a turbulent inland ocean with vicious waves.

THE ORIGIN OF HIPPOS
A myth from the Orikara Patri-Clan of Elmolo

A long long time ago, back when animals could talk, the hippopotamuses were the cows of the Elmolo. These cows had no teeth and had to be fed by hand. There was a man who had two wives. One wife looked after the goats (which were crocodiles), and the other looked after the cows (the hippos). A corral was built on Lorian Island to keep the cows inside.

One day when the husband left to go fishing, the woman who looked after the cows became very thirsty. She said, "Cows of my husband, fetch me some water in my calabash." At first the cows refused. Then they agreed, but only if she would open the corral very wide.

The cows immediately ran away into the water to Lentarit. The woman called to them to come back, but they would not listen. She felt very bad, and prayed to Elwak (god) to help the cows eat so they would not starve. Elwak heard her, and that was how the hippos got teeth.

When her husband returned home, he found the corral empty. He called the cows by their names, but they would not come back. He said to his wife, "Just leave them. They will eventually return, for they know I am their keeper." They waited a long time, but the cows never came back. That is why when the Elmolo men wish to hunt hippos, they must go to the head of the family of Orikara. His family were the first keepers of the hippo; only he knows the prayers and blessings for a good hunt.

Scattered at various sites in the Chalbi Desert are several springs that support the doum palm, a plant that provides essential raw materials for the Elmolo. The trunks are used as logs for fishing rafts. The palm fronds form covering for their huts, and the fiber is extracted for making rope and string. The doum palm also bears fruit, a kind of date called *loka*, which is the people's second basic food. The loka has a brown rind that is ground and used as a substitute for corn flour. The ripe nut contains a refreshing milk and a small kernel that is soft and tasty.

The lake teems with fish and crocodiles. The largest fish is the enormous Nile perch, which can weigh up to 200 pounds. Although less numerous than in the past, the hippopotamus can still be seen north of Loiyangalani. The lake shore used to support many other animals such as zebra, elephant, lesser kudu, giraffe, rhino, and oryx. Some of these animals, for instance the elephant, have long since fallen victim to poachers, people who hunt illegally. Lions have moved farther north along the shore. Water birds continue to be plentiful. Venomous snakes and scorpions inhabit the shrub and sand.

The hippopotamus, the most significant animal in Elmolo culture and ritual, is now found farther north, near Moite Hill. The hides of these animals are used for making sandals, which are in great demand by neighboring peoples.▲

chapter

3

HISTORY AND TRADITION

LITTLE IS KNOWN ABOUT THE ELMOLO BEFORE the 1880s. No written record existed until European explorers reached the Lake Turkana region and began to describe the various peoples they encountered.

Very few Europeans actually met any Elmolo. One of these expeditions reached Lake Turkana in 1895, and another in 1903. Both expeditions recorded in their journals that these people lived in huts on islands and mostly ate fish, with occasional turtle, crocodile, and hippo meat. To catch their food, they used log rafts, harpoons, and fishing nets.

The Europeans and the Elmolo could not understand each other. They could only communicate two words, *kushumba,* "white man," and *tambac,* "tobacco."

The Elmolo use rafts as one method of catching fish. The fish are then cut into long strips and dried in the sun.

KENYA: COLONIALISM AND INDEPENDENCE

The Elmolo are unusual because they have not been so much affected as other East African peoples by political changes in Kenya. To understand their world, however, it is important to know what has happened to it throughout the last century.

In 1895 Great Britain took over Kenya as a colony. Many expensive cash crops such as coffee and palm oil could be grown in the more fertile parts of Kenya. Problems arose when the British demanded only the best land for raising their expensive crops. Many native groups, such as the farming Agikuyu and the cattle-raising Maasai, were already living on the fertile land. The British forced these peoples to move to reservations, where the land was dry and there was not enough space. The good land was given to European settlers, who were supposed to grow crops for British profit. This is similar to what happened to Native Americans when people of European stock took over their lands and forced them onto reservations.

As more native farmers were forced off their land and more pastoralists were forced to sell their cattle, the people of Kenya began to fight back. After World War II a movement called Mau Mau called for reform and protested with violence. The British put down this radical movement by 1952, but less violent groups continued the struggle. By the end of 1963 Kenya had won its independence from Britain and formed its own new government.

The problems faced by Kenya's native peoples did not end with independence. The new government was interested in "progress," just as the British had been. Many of the same policies that had threatened traditional practices were continued in the new era. Children are still encouraged to get a modern education; farmers and pastoralists are taught modern techniques for using the land. For the Elmolo, the idea of competition and money has become more important than traditional values of communal sharing.

It is difficult for old customs to stand up against modern ideas. The Elmolo are facing this problem now, as the island settlement follows traditions and the mainland settlement explores new practices. There is good in both of these approaches. The challenge is to be a part of the future without losing touch with the past.

▼ EUROPEAN VISITORS ▼

Although the British colonial government had been in control of the territory since 1895, the Elmolo were not visited again by Europeans until Dyson and Fuchs reported on their exploration of the area in 1934. The history of most native Kenyan peoples was affected greatly by the presence and control of the British. Because the Elmolo were hunters and fishers and very few in number, they gained little attention from the colonial government.

The colonial government did try to protect the Elmolo from raiders who swept down from the north and northeast. They established a police post at Loiyangalani in 1911 but abandoned it in 1915. Only after World War I, in 1921, was it reestablished.

Loiyangalani, the site of a number of ancient springs and groves of doum palm, had been a spot where various groups had come since time immemorial to water their animals or obtain raw materials. The Elmolo visited the area regularly to obtain doum palm logs for their rafts, fronds for their shelters, and fiber for rope. They also collected the *loka* fruit.

In 1934 the Elmolo were living in "beehive-shaped grass huts" in two villages. One of these was on a rocky island offshore, the other on a sandpit in Elmolo Bay. Because of the lowering of the water level, only one island was left to inhabit. Both villages were of the same people, and individuals continually moved between the two sites. When living on the island, the women were not permitted to cross to the mainland. There was only one headman, who lived in the island village.

▼ LIFESTYLES ▼

The Elmolo employed three methods of fishing: harpooning, netting, and hook-and-line fishing. The harpoon was also used in hunting crocodiles and hippos. Both animals were attacked on land, never in the water. Hippo hunts occurred very rarely; they took place at night shortly after the rains, when the hippos came ashore to graze on the new grass. Hook-and-line fishing was used to catch Nile perch and water tortoises.

Important implements were log rafts, harpoons, nets, cutting and piercing implements made from oryx horns, and pottery.

The Elmolo mode of dress was minimal. Men wore a waist string of alternate glass beads and fish vertebrae. Bracelets made from the skin of the water tortoise, rings, and necklaces of iron were common adornments. Feather hair ornaments were also used. Sandals made from hippo hides completed the outfit. The usual dress for women was the *selah*, a type of skirt consisting of overlapping rear and front pieces of netting.

An Elmolo fisherman with a characteristic harpoon.

The women wore many ornaments of brass or iron wire on their arms and as earrings. Large numbers of necklaces of ostrich-shell beads and trade beads were worn around the neck and head.

The Elmolo were a cooperative society. Food was shared among all, including those who could not help in fishing or hunting. They were monogamous (had only one wife at a time) and married only within their own people. They lived in nuclear households consisting of a couple and their children, not more than three.

In 1934 Dyson and Fuchs counted only 84 Elmolo men, women, and children, down from perhaps 200 a few decades earlier.

Pictured here are an Elmolo mother wearing ornaments, and a young girl depicting a typical Elmolo hairstyle.

The Elmolo have had to invent medical practices to help them handle health problems caused by their environment, poor diet, and inbreeding. Lake Turkana is very high in a chemical called alkaline. When alkaline meets with calcium, the calcium dissolves. For many decades, all their food and drink have come from the lake, so they have consumed large quantities of alkaline from childhood. The result of this has been painful bone and tooth diseases in almost every member of the group.

▼ ORIGINS ▼

On the basis of years of historical, cultural, and linguistic research, it is now believed that the Elmolo were a splinter group of the Rendille and that their original language was a version of a Rendille dialect. They migrated south sometime in the 1500s from what is now Ethiopia. In the intervening centuries, they lived in relative isolation from other groups and therefore developed their own language and culture. It is significant, however, that the Boran, the Rendille, and the Elmolo all believe in Wak as the supreme being. The Elmolo, like the Rendille, bury their dead in stone cairns. This view of the origin of the Elmolo people is in keeping with the stories told by Elmolo elders, who maintain that they are distinct and not related in any way to any of the surrounding tribes.

The neighboring Samburu have had a decisive effect on Elmolo culture. This influence dates back to the 1880s and '90s when drought struck and a devastating epidemic of rinderpest broke out among the Samburu cattle, wiping out most of their herds. The cattle-herders, being without stock, could not survive. They looked to the Elmolo, who lived by hunting and fishing, and forced the Elmolo to accept them in their midst and to speak the Samburu language.

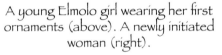
A young Elmolo girl wearing her first ornaments (above). A newly initiated woman (right).

▼ SAMBURU INFLUENCES ▼

The organization of Samburu society is quite different from that of the Elmolo. The Samburu, like many other African peoples, have an initiated class of young men called *murran*, or warriors. Their function is to protect the community from raiders and to raid other peoples for cattle. The Elmolo have no equivalent to the *murran* class, recognizing instead the successful hippo hunter as cultural hero. The Elmolo were in a

time of crisis when the Samburu joined them.
They were intimidated by the Samburu warriors.
The Samburu presented themselves as superior
and worthy of emulation. Their influence was so
great that the Elmolo even began speaking the
Samburu language. Over the course of this
century, the traditional Elmolo language has
been mostly forgotten, although Elmolo speech
still contains many old words related to fishing,
hunting, and raft- and harpoon-making for
which Samburu had no words.

Despite the loss of their language, the Elmolo
have tenaciously held onto other fundamental
aspects of their culture such as fishing. European
influence began in 1962 when the British colonial
government forced the Elmolo to leave their
islands and settle near Loiyangalani, where a
new police post had been erected for protection
of the residents. The immediate cause of this
government intervention was drought and
Somali raiders looking for food. The split in
Elmolo society between mainland and island
groups dates to this time.

The Consolata Fathers established a Catholic
mission at Loiyangalani in 1965, and Elmolo
men helped in the construction of the buildings.
They were paid in cloth, fat, and maize-meal.
Adults and children began to wear European
clothing, which they obtained from the mission,
and women wore skirts in the presence of

priests. A school building was completed in 1968, and a few children began to attend the mission school, mainly because they were given free food if they went. In time, Elmolo parents learned about the Catholic God from their children, and a number of parents began attending Mass on Sunday; a few have been baptized. Because a patient once died at the new Mission Dispensary (hospital), few Elmolo go there when they are sick.▲

chapter

4

CONTEMPORARY
CUSTOMS AND RITUALS

THE ELMOLO OF TODAY CONTINUE TO LIVE IN
their two settlements by the lake. Over the years,
their population has increased: from 84 in 1934,
to 143 in 1958, to 233 in 1973. A principal
explanation for the relatively small population is
their diet and the health problems associated
with it. Life expectancy is short. People usually
live only to 35 or 45 years, resulting in fewer
childbearing years. Women and newborns have
a high mortality rate, as do men engaged in
dangerous fishing and hunting activities. Several
social customs also keep the population low. For
example, a person who has been widowed is not
allowed to remarry. The Elmolo consider the
birth of twins a misfortune, and the second-born
twin is usually killed.

In recent years, the Elmolo diet has improved, and in a few instances men from other

An Elmolo woman builds her hut, following the Samburu method.

groups have married Elmolo women. These developments may cause the population to keep growing.

The mainland village, near Loiyanglani, is the larger one. It contains 49 households with a total of 184 people. The island settlement has 13 households and a population of only 49. It practices a more traditional culture, living off the lake, supplemented once in a while by hippo and crocodile hunts, although hippos are now rare in the area.

▼ THE FAMILY ▼
In both settlements, the household is the nuclear family made up of husband, wife, and

unmarried children. Each married male has his
own hut in which he lives with his wife and children. A newly married couple usually build their
hut close to the husband's kin. Traditionally the
Elmolo practice endogamy. This is the custom of
marrying only members of one's own ethnic
group. It is breaking down in the Loiyangalani
community, however, from which three Elmolo
women have married Samburu men, one a
Rendille man, and one a Turkana. No Elmolo
man has ever married a woman from outside his
group.

The Elmolo build their dwellings in the traditional manner. The hut is constructed of a
center pole and palm fronds placed in a circle
several yards from the pole. The fronds are bent
inward and attached to the pole. The huts are
low, and entrances are only three feet high.
These dwellings provide sleeping space, shelter
from sun and heat, storage for supplies, and a
cooking place. Most of the day is spent out-
doors. The huts of the village are arranged in a
semicircle, and the space enclosed by them is
cleared and serves as a communal area.

▼ THE WORKDAY ▼

Most activities in the villages are divided
between men and women. Only a few tasks
are shared by both genders. Girls help their
mothers, and boys assist their fathers when not

Elderly women help in many areas, including making rope and taking care of the children. Boys learn fishing skills like harpooning.

engaged in their own play activities. Elderly women help with child care, household chores, and making rope, while elderly men make nets and implements or just sit playing Ntototi, a favorite board game.

The people's staple food is fish, occasionally supplemented by crocodile and goat meat. Everyone helps with fishing, and the methods used are essentially unchanged from decades ago. Rafts, harpoons, spears, nets, and hook-and-line are the most important implements. Men make all the tools used in hunting, fishing, and defense. Women focus on housekeeping, building and repairing the huts, supplying water,

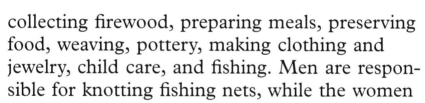

collecting firewood, preparing meals, preserving food, weaving, pottery, making clothing and jewelry, child care, and fishing. Men are responsible for knotting fishing nets, while the women twist the twine and rope.

Although traditionally groups of Elmolo men did net-fishing, women now take part in it. Net-fishing is usually done in the afternoon, and on nights when the moon is between one half and one quarter full. Everyone, including children, engages in hook-and-line fishing from rocks along the shore.

Only adult men, perhaps accompanied by adolescent sons, go on crocodile hunts. The animals are ensnared in ropes and then harpooned in the shallows of the lake.

With the influx of outsiders and the influence of the mission, the mode of dress has changed. In the mainland village, all but the very young and old have adopted some form of European dress. Women wear skirts and blouses, and men wear shorts or trousers.

This is not so in the island community, where women continue to wear the *selah*, especially when out fishing. The men wear cloth wrapped around the waist.

▼ THE CLANS ▼

The Elmolo are divided into five clans, each named for a male ancestor. Relationships to this ancestor cannot be established in a direct line. Children are automatically assigned to the clan of their father. Each of the five clans has a totem, or special animal that it considers a symbol of the clan's identity. Surrounding each totem is a set of taboos and prohibitions, particular rules of behavior designed to keep bad luck away. The Orikara clan is associated with the hippopotamus and is the only clan with an origin story. Members of this clan may not eat tigerfish or hippo calves. The Orikala totem is the mudfish; members may not eat the tail end of certain kinds of fish, nor are they allowed to eat camel meat or to touch camels. The Lmaryle are associated with the Nile perch and are prohibited from eating crocodile or turtles. The Orikaya are associated with the tigerfish, and the Orisiole with birds.

Each clan has a headman who also acts as a priest, performing certain religious ceremonies. The Orikara clan headman conducts prayers before a hippo hunt. The head of the mudfish clan is the expert in infertility, and the head of the Nile perch clan prays for rain. Numerous taboos regulate the behavior of clan members, since breaking any one of them brings misfortune to the individual and his community.

South of Lorian Island is the island of Waar, site of the sacred shrines of the Elmolo. All clans except the Orikaya maintain sacred huts on Waar

Island. Clan heads go there from time to time to maintain the shrines and to pray. The Elmolo believe in one supreme being, Wak. In their belief system they find meaning in all kinds of natural and human phenomena. They also fear harm from sorcerers from other peoples.

Group decisions are made by a council, which includes all married male members of the community. One headman directs the council. The council decides on serious disputes and rule-breaking in the community. For minor problems, the Elmolo have a unique way of letting a person know that he or she has mis-behaved without the necessity of confrontation. A member of the council sings a song about the wrongdoing so that the miscreant can hear it. A song such as this may be composed only by someone of the same sex as the miscreant. The two sexes are often separated in Elmolo tradi-tion. For example, the hair of a young boy can be cut only by a man, and the hair of a girl only by a woman.

▼ LIFE STAGES ▼

Important life events in Elmolo society are birth, puberty, courtship, marriage, and death. The mother and newborn are considered par-ticularly vulnerable. For the first four days after giving birth, a new mother is not allowed to cook or even eat any food. She may only drink

water that has been flavored by boiling dried
fish in it. Woman and child remain secluded for
several days after birth. Once the child has
focused its eyes and can follow a hand moved in
front of its face, it is brought out to show to the
proud father.

Puberty among girls is marked by a ceremony, after which the girl's new status as
woman is publicly announced. For boys, this
transition is less marked in Elmolo society, but a
few young men have chosen to undergo the
Samburu circumcision rites at this time in life.

After adolescence, girls are closely watched.
There are few chances for a young man to
develop a friendship with a young woman.
Courtship, therefore, develops slowly. When a
young man becomes interested in a young
woman, he makes his intention known to his
parents. If the choice is acceptable to them,
negotiations for the brideprice begin. Bride-
wealth or brideprice is a common practice
among East African peoples. It is a quantity of
goods or livestock that the groom must pay to
his bride's family for the privilege of marrying
her. If all goes well, the groom may live with his
bride after he has paid a portion of the bride
price. The couple may live together for up to a
year on a trial basis. At a certain time during
this period, the families of the couple decide
that they should now be married for good,

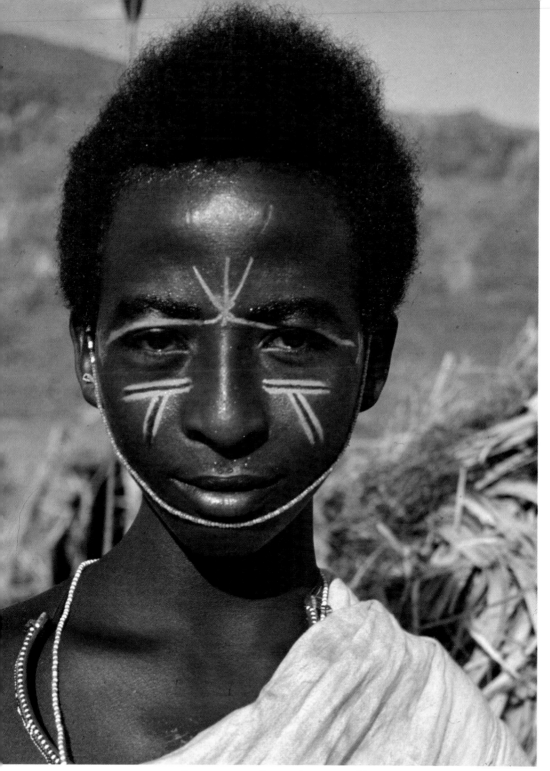

Face decorations of a newly initiated boy.

An elder walking on the shore of Lake Turkana.

and an elaborate marriage ceremony is held. After this, the marriage is final and cannot be dissolved.

Elmolo people die young. A man over 41 years old is considered an elder. Children are expected to take care of their infirm parents. The Elmolo believe that at death the person's soul returns to Wak. The soul, in the form of a white cloudlike shape, may appear in people's dreams for good or evil. Good luck as well as misfortune are attributed to these spirits. Burial of a dead person takes place during the day in a grave about a foot deep. Each relative and friend of the deceased places a rock on top of the body, making a stone cairn approximately three feet high. From the time of burial the dead person's name may never again be spoken.

▼ THE HIPPO HUNT ▼

Another important event in Elmolo life is the annual hippo hunt, the *njore*. The hippopotamus is surrounded by a mythical aura. The date of the hunt is set by the elders in consultation with the headman of the Orikara hippo clan. The men of the hunting party spend several days preparing their harpoons, rafts, and rope. One day is spent in prayer and ceremonial singing at the Orikara shrine on Waar Island. Having prepared themselves physically and spiritually, the men move north toward Moite Hill. Having located a group of hippos, the men carefully plan their attack. In a cooperative manner they surround one animal, and exactly at the right moment the men closest to the animal throw their harpoons at their target. They try to hit the animal as close to shore as possible, since they would have little chance of bringing it to land from deeper waters. If the harpoons reach their mark, the ropes are used to drag the animal to shore. This is no easy task, since an adult hippo weighs more than four tons and has huge tusklike teeth that can tear a man to pieces. The stuggle between the men and the hippo may therefore take several hours. Once the carcass is on land, the man who threw the first spear is declared the killer of the hippo. He receives the tail, ears, and tongue of the animal, which he attaches to his harpoon as a sign of his accomplishment. The carcass is then butchered and the meat transported back to the village. The returning men give thanks in song and prayer to Wak and to the hippo for giving his life. Celebration of the successful hunt lasts for several days. Only on the day after the hunters' return is the hippo killer allowed to eat hippo meat. His throwing arm is decorated with sacred white chalk, and a special earring made from a hippo bone is placed in his right ear. This earring is worn for life.

Hippo hunts are serious business. It is quite common for hunters to be badly injured or even killed by an enraged animal. The hippo hunt of the Elmolo is a unique occasion; nothing comparable is found in neighboring societies. It is organized by the island community, but people from the mainland settlement may participate in the event.▲

chapter

5

DAILY LIFE

A TYPICAL DAY IN THE ISLAND VILLAGE BEGINS at daybreak before sunrise. People start to stir in their huts; some sleepy-eyed children appear. Dogs get up from their resting place to look for a meal. The day ahead will be filled with many varied activities, most of them directly related to the people's personal and group survival. Only a few items can be obtained from the town store by trading. Everything else the people need to live they manufacture themselves. Little is wasted or thrown away.

As people rise, their sleeping mats are rolled up and moved out of the way to the edge of the hut. In D'o's hut, her first task is to see after her youngest child, two-year-old Logontok. Then she prepares a meal of fish and maize-meal porridge. As she does this, she checks her supplies of dried fish, *loka* fruit, and maize-meal

The killer of the hippo is honored as a hero.

stored in baskets toward the back of the hut.
She is out of doum palm fronds, but she and a
few other women will go to the oasis today
to gather a new supply. In the gourd by the
entrance, some goat milk is left from the night
before. Enough for breakfast. But the water pot
is empty. D'o sends her older daughter, Ngeta,
to fetch water from the lake.

Breakfast over, any remaining embers from
the cooking fire are carefully put out, and
leftover scraps of food are tossed to the few

yellow dogs waiting patiently nearby. Yi, D'o's husband, joins the other men who have gathered in the village clearing to talk about good fishing sites, and to discuss the strength and direction of the wind. A group of young boys go exploring for turtle and crocodile eggs, small game, and birds.

D'o, Logontok on her back, and Ngeta meet the other two women and their sons who want to make the seven-mile trek to the oasis today. The sun has only just appeared on the horizon, and the small group walks relatively easily in the cool of the morning.

Meanwhile, several of the men have decided to go spear-fishing for Nile perch. Parr and his eleven-year-old son, Cai, go down to the landing to load their raft with two harpoon spears and extra rope. Other men do the same nearby.

Twenty-eight-year-old Yi and his younger brother, Jike, want to hunt crocodile today. They know a spot where crocodile like to lie on warm rocks by the shore. They choose several heavier harpoons and rope for their équipment. Having made their fishing and hunting plans for the day, the men move off in small groups in different directions.

Next to D'o's hut, Kia, D'o's sister, is pounding some palm leaves into string, and an elderly woman is weaving a sitting mat. While their hands are busy, they tell stories and visit with each other.

▼ AT THE OASIS ▼

By midmorning, D'o and her party have arrived at the grove of palm trees. The boys climb the trees and cut fronds; seven or eight for each woman. The bottoms of the palm fronds are cut off and they are thoroughly wetted and stacked, making a bundle easily carried on the woman's back. The women and children collect any *loka* fruit they find and tie them in a cloth bundle. While at the oasis, one of the women trades a small pot for a bag of maize-meal with a relative who lives in the settlement. The women do not linger at the oasis, but soon start on the return trip to avoid the scorching heat later in the day. The palm fronds would be useless for making rope if they dried out. While D'o carries her bundle of palm fronds, Ngeta carries her little brother, Logontok.

As the heat becomes more intense, Kia tires of rope-making and sends word to several of her friends to go net-fishing in the lake. The children are excited at this prospect, since it will give them a chance to play in the water. Five women with their nets, knives, and extra rope move off toward the spot that has been pointed out by Kia's grandfather as the best for net-fishing on this day. The children follow along. The women enter the water, form a half circle, and spread the nets between them. The children beat the water at the open end of the circle and

Men clean and scale the day's catch.

drive the fish into the nets amid shouts and much commotion. Fish caught in the net are killed and threaded on rope hanging from a woman's waist.

After an hour or so, enough fish have been caught. Each fish is cleaned and carried back to the village. Part of the catch is distributed to parents and friends. Fish are selected for the evening meal of stew. Any fish left over is cut into strips and dried.

Immediately after her return from Loiyangalani, D'o begins working on the new palm fronds. She starts pounding the palm leaves into fiber. Ngeta helps by wetting the leaves. They then twist the fiber into twine and rope.

▼ HOME FROM THE HUNT ▼

In the late afternoon, some of the men return with their rafts, each with at least something to show for the day's labor. Some have long ropes of threaded fish. Neither Parr and his son, Cai,

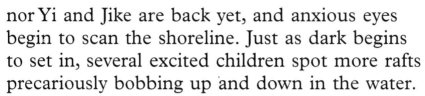

nor Yi and Jike are back yet, and anxious eyes begin to scan the shoreline. Just as dark begins to set in, several excited children spot more rafts precariously bobbing up and down in the water.

As the rafts come closer, a huge fish is seen tied to Parr's raft. Yi and Jike's raft rides low in the water, indicating a heavy load. The people are joyful and help pull the rafts up on shore. Parr and Cai have caught a very large Nile perch. Excitedly, they tell the onlookers of how they fought with the fish for several hours before it finally could be brought alongside the raft.

Yi and Jike tell how they slowly sneaked up on a group of crocodiles from downwind. By working together, they were able to isolate one of the creatures and harpoon it with two of their spears. Because of their skill, the ropes were attached securely but the crocodile did not give up easily. With much emotion, Jike told how the animal had struggled ferociously in its attempt to free itself. Holding onto the ropes and countering the crocodile's movements from different directions, Yi and Jike had battled with it for a very long time. At last, the crocodile had tired and the men could move in closer. When it was safe, its enormous jaws had been tied shut with the extra rope. The tail was cut off. Then it was skinned and cut up, and its meat loaded onto the raft.

Everyone agrees that Yi and Jike must be very

skillful indeed to have subdued an animal big enough to give as much meat as was lying on the raft. Even smaller crocodiles than this one usually take three or four men to bring down.

It has been a good day. Everyone receives a share of the fish and crocodile meat. The people are grateful that none of their friends has been hurt or lost. They give thanks and start to prepare the evening meal. The aroma of fish stew and roasted crocodile fills the air.

The evening meal is a leisurely affair. People sit by their huts in small family groups, exchanging stories. Subdued laughter can be heard here and there. As the light fades rapidly, fires are lit. The men talk about the possibility of rain. Past triumphs are recalled and future ventures are anticipated. Later the people begin to sing and dance as they do every night when the moon is between half and completely full. Young men and women steal glances at each other in the moonlight. Yes, it has been a good day. ★▲

★ This account of daily life among the Elmolo is adapted, in part, from Joann Carole Scherrer's ethnography, *Fisherfolk of the Desert.*

chapter

6

A VIEW OF
THE FUTURE

THE ELMOLO ARE SURVIVING AS A PEOPLE.
Their growing population shows that. In other
respects, however, their culture has undergone
continuous change throughout this century.

Their close association with the Samburu
introduced the Elmolo to the raising of animals
in addition to fishing and hunting. Although the
Elmolo preferred small stock such as goats and
sheep, some now also raise cattle. In addition,
they have intermarried with the Samburu,
Turkana, and Rendille, and this has introduced
new elements into Elmolo culture.

As Elmolo women marry Samburu and
Turkana men, they become subject to the
marriage rules of these groups. Through inter-
marriage, the Elmolo clans can now claim relationships with the Samburu, Rendille, and
Turkana. This close association has also led to

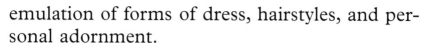

emulation of forms of dress, hairstyles, and personal adornment.

Other influences on the Elmolo are their contact with government officials, Europeans, and the Christian mission. The Elmolo have settled near the Loiyangalani government post. This location has increased their contact with other cultural groups. The Elmolo also observed the lifestyles of the Europeans. In time they were introduced to working for money wages. Some Elmolo children have learned to read and write at the mission school. A few families have been baptized.

A significant event occurred in 1973 when thousands of scientists, tourists, and journalists descended on Loiyangalani to observe the solar eclipse. A lodge was built to accommodate the visitors. Elmolo worked on the construction and later as employees at the lodge. For the first time, they experienced the use of money as a medium of exchange. Tourists in particular paid exorbitantly for services in money, clothing, food, watches, radios, lighters, and so on.

▼ THE PROFIT MOTIVE ▼

The introduction of money began the breakdown of the Elmolo cooperative system. Traditionally any goods obtained by an individual were distributed equally among the Elmolo clans. Individuals now wanted to keep their earnings for themselves. The conflict is particularly noticeable in the small general store, *duka*, which dispenses staples such as maize-meal, sugar, fat, tobacco, cloth, tea, and a type of home-brew beer. Meals are also served at this store, which has become a meeting place for Elmolo, Samburu, Rendille, and Turkana tribesmen. The *duka* now sells goods, instead of sharing or exchanging them in the traditional Elmolo way.

As a consequence of the various influences on them, the Elmolo now have choices of how to live and what to believe. As individuals, they can work for wages, follow a pastoralist lifestyle, or remain fishermen. It is unlikely that the Elmolo will give up fishing as an important source of food. The small town of Loiyangalani does not provide opportunities for all. Scarce grazing and periodic drought conditions in the area do not allow a complete changeover from a fishing to a herding existence.

The Elmolo therefore continue to fish and hunt even while they learn other lifestyles. However, as long as people fish on Lake Turkana, they will need the skills and vocabulary associated with this activity. Even now, the Elmolo still use at least five different words for water to describe the variable conditions of the lake. They also have at least eight words for wind, expressing differences from "light breeze" to "howling gale." This aspect of Elmolo language and culture will survive as long as these people live by the windy Lake Turkana.▲

Glossary

anthropologist Scientist who studies the origins and lifestyles of human societies.

cairn Burial mound made of stones piled on the dead body.

culture The ways of life established by a group of human beings and handed down through generations.

endogamy Practice that restricts marriage to a certain social unit (traditionally an Elmolo must marry another Elmolo, not someone from another ethnic group).

fossil The imprint or remains of a living organism, such as a bone, shell, or leaf print.

gura paua "People of the Lake," the Elmolo traditional name for themselves.

Jade Sea Europeans' nickname for Lake Turkana, because of its intense color.

loka Fruit of the doum palm, a staple in the Elmolo diet.

monogamy The practice of having only one spouse at a time.

pastoralist Member of a society that makes its living through herding of animals.

polygamy Having two or more wives, common among many African peoples.

oasis Fertile area in a desert or arid region, usually fed by a spring (Loiyangalani is the oasis near the larger Elmolo settlement).

selah woman's skirt, made of netting.

taboo Activity that is not allowed by a society because it is thought to be bad luck.

Wak The creator of life in traditional Elmolo religion.

For Further Reading

Dyson, W.S. and Fuchs, V.E. "The Elmolo," *Journal of the Royal Anthropological Institute*, vol. 67, pp. 327–342, 1937.

Hoehnel, Ludwig von. *Discovery by Count Teleki of Lakes Rudolf and Stefanie*, 2 vol. London: Longmans, Green, 1894.

Leaky, Richard E. "In Search of Man's Past at Lake Rudolf." *National Geographic*, Vol. 137, No. 5, pp. 712–733, May 1970.

——. "Skull 1470." *National Geographic*, vol. 143, No. 6, pp. 819–289, June 1973.

Pavitt, Nigel. *Kenya: The First Explorers*. London: Aurum Press, 1989.

Scherrer, Joann Carole. "Fisherfolk of the Desert: An Ethnography of the Elmolo of Kenya," Anthropological PhD Dissertation, University of Virginia, 1978.

Sobiana, Neal. "Fishermen Herders: Subsistence, Survival, and Cultural Change in Northern Kenya." *Journal of African History*, vol. 29, pp. 41–56, 1988.

Index

ABOUT THE AUTHOR

Ursula R. Gaertner is a sociologist who studied in England and the United States. She received a Ph.D. from Case Western Reserve University in Cleveland, Ohio. Her special interest is in comparative social institutions. She has lived in Europe, among the Elmolo of Kenya, and elsewhere.

PHOTO CREDITS: CFM, Nairobi
DESIGN: Kim Sonsky